Roads Taken

Bruce Louis Dodson

ISBN: 978-93-95224-15-4

First Edition: 2022
Rs. 200/-

Cyberwit.net
HIG 45 Kaushambi Kunj, Kalindipuram
Allahabad - 211011 (U.P.) India
http://www.cyberwit.net
Tel: +(91) 9415091004
E-mail: info@cyberwit.net

Contents

Free Concert

Sunday in the park
September - San Francisco
Band Shell orchestra
Beneath the last of warming suns
Conductor taps his wand
Preparing for the anthem
Some stand
But others are too old, or tired.

The anthem blares
A flock of pigeons flare above
They know the score
Time to move on.

The act of leaving home is easier
Than being the departed from.

Hong Kong

Kowloon - Chungking Mansions
Third world Casablanca
Smell of spices and fried foods
Rise from first-floor farmers markets
Jewelry on the cheap
Watches and cell phones
Might last for a week . . . three if you're lucky.
Labyrinth of aisles and warrens
Maze of small shops
Harried clerks and throngs of customers
Newspapers from a world of nations
Money changers
Foods for any taste
Illumination is forever fluorescent
High noon to midnight.

There's an edgy, gritty feel
Above all this
Some twenty floors of mom and pop one-star hotels
Rest stops for immigrants and new arrivals
Lonely Planet tourists
Travelers of low means.
A constant rattle of Mahjong tiles echo in the air shaft at my window
Looking out on other rooms the same as mine
The price is right
Stay here a day or two at most.

On my way out this early morning
Passing still closed shops
The biggest rat I've ever seen.

Brazil

Side walking - Rio de Janeiro

Humble altars set by fire plugs, stop signs . . . tree trunks
Dusty candles stuck in cola bottlenecks along the curbside
Flicker nervously beside the evening traffic
Scent of ethanol exhaust and lipstick
Cigarettes are left
A bit of candy
Shiny coins—still new
Unspendable
Made worthless by spectacular inflation . . . time and place.
Small offerings to spirit gods displaced by fire and greed
Their forests gone forever
Forced to live upon the streets of Rio de Janeiro
With believers
Sleeping in favellas or the city's esplanades.

These ancient spirit gods are angry
They will have revenge.

Yemanja

A night in Buzios, Brazil
Warm sea breeze comes ashore
Caressing . . . sultry breath of oceans.
Fishing boats rock gently on the dark horizon
Flashlights blinking in the distance from on board
As crews make ready for the coming day.
They call the sea Yemanja here
She is alive
A personality with changing moods that beckon those on land
With playfulness
The promise of adventure
Rolls within the sound of crashing waves
        Do not forsake me
        There is no good reason for a man to leave the sea
        I'm everything you want
        Your greatest love
        Both life and death
        All things between.
Her implorations spill from arms that want to hold
Forever...
Cool wet shadow slipping through the sand
Returning to drowned lovers.

India

Benares

Ganges early morning
Sun comes pale pink
Rising out of dust horizon
Long warm days before monsoon.
Stone and concrete reflect the day's new light
Gold temple tops cast daytime stars onto this timeless river.

Dugouts float past, barely moving
Oars creak
Temple bells are tolling
Voices over water . . . hushed.
A trail of laundrymen beat shirts, and sheets and saris
Against rocks worn smooth so many lives ago

No one remembers.
Songs and whopping echo down this holy river.
Krishna! Whop. Om Shanti! Whop. Jai Rama! Whop.

Vultures soar patiently above
Without a trace of effort
Glide through pale blue fog mist
Above the burning ghats
Along the shore
The end and the beginning.

Oarsman - Benares

Creaking oarlocks take us out
Into the pale fog mist
This sacred river
Ganges.

I am with an ancient oarsman
Rowing slowly . . . without effort
Drifting with the current

Muddy vein of life
Unending
Mother of the world.
Great cities come and go along the shore
He tells me
Mighty temples rise up over centuries
Adoring God
Then fall to earth
Forsaken by him
As this river flows into forever.

Steam Engine – Tamil Nadu to Benares

Cavernous station echoes . . . Chaiiii!
The hiss of steam
Great massive beast at rest
Soot blackened
Heavy chuff of idling power
As we board in thrilled anticipation
First class, private sleeper
Gray steel walls hold fold-down beds
A 1940's battleship decor.

Lurch into motion
We begin to pick up speed
The easy, rhythmic, track-born clatter

Windows open to the heated day
Dogs watch our passing
Hopefully await
Unwanted lunches tossed away.

Infrequent villages appear to punctuate
Vast empty spaces, treeless
Film strip passing images
Are irresistibly romantic
Lust entwined
That iron bed remembered still
As India unfolded
On that endless day
Trip of a lifetime.

Oh, that I could take that ride again.

Tiruchirappalli -Tamil Nadu

Morning comes
The only difference here from night
Is light
As life goes on all hours
The nights are cooler than the sun-bleached days.

The town is self-described, industrial
With endless slums of palm leaf shanties
Darkened from years of dust and smoke
Reduced to shades of black and tan
The unpaved streets are filled with human forms and animals.

They start out early
Wheelwrights, potters, weavers, fortune tellers
Rickshaws, cows, and businessmen in shabby brown suits
Office workers.
Labor stops at noon
With sun directly overhead
Equator's shimmering, deadly heat
A starving dog finds a convenient place to die.

At three the pace picks up again
Increasing with the length of early evening shadows
Life begins to seem more possible
Another day has been survived
Tomorrow will be much the same
One wonders, was it ever so?

Up from this sunbaked earth
Impossible stone monoliths extend
From long past years
Into a timeless sky
As if to grasp unseen immortals
Above entrances to temple labyrinths.
More than a hundred priests attend as many alters
Waiting for the seekers of improvement
Who trod barefoot across stones worn smooth
By ancestors, their fathers, father's, fathers.
Sculptured deities in every corner
Some are crumbling and ignored
Almost forgotten in these modern times.

Both gods and demons find their last abode in Trichy.
Land of fortune tellers, jungles, spells, and curses
White men feel oppressed here
Weak
Subdued
Exhausted
Out of touch within this other world.

Nepal

In Kathmandu

Rain falls like Shiva's tears
Great darkened clouds
Come roiling down from jagged peaks
Above the valley
Thunder echoes
Lightning scatters monkeys
Who take shelter in the wooden eves above an ancient temple
As umbrellas blossom in the marketplace below.
Monsoon.

Germany

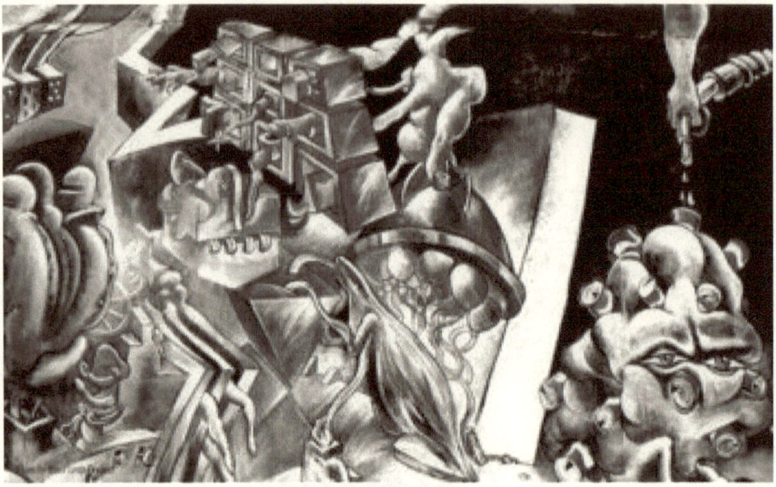

Walls

They only stand a while
Contrived to separate
Describing boundaries
Stone and concrete
Still . . .
None last forever.

In the meantime
They are unimaginary
And expensive
Causing separation, pain, and want
Both sides
    What reason?
        Who decided?

Berlin's wall
Stood over twenty years
More than a hundred lost their lives
Attempting crossing
One side to the other.

Tumbled now
Fractured remains have become souvenirs
People buy chunks of it in shops
That lay in wait
At what was Checkpoint Charlie
Where a last part of the wall remains to serve
As concrete canvas for its spray-paint artwork
Names of passers-by names and comments
On this grim memorial.

Some sections have been whitewashed
And now re-graffitied by professionals
Fine artists born on either side
In celebration of its fall.

New images evoke remembrance of the wall that was.
Others remain
Beyond the reach of sight and unencumbered
By the weight of mass:
The walls of class and race
Between the rich and poor
And others we build around ourselves
Our neighbors
Nations
Lovers
Children.

Some who dared
Attempted crossing over
Others simply waited
For the day when walls would disappear
Knowing their inbred failure:
Reason for existence
And high maintenance
The cost.

Traveling by Sea — The Dangers

Engine failure:
Due to flooding
Cause unknown
Bad maintenance
A faulty pump.
No autopsy at fifty fathoms.

Deadheads:
Running into floating objects
Things that shouldn't be there.
Operator fell asleep
Controls and course preset
While still in safety of the harbor
Ocean, smooth and flat
With splatterings of moonlight
Ship on autopilot
Late night, engine humming softly.
Helmsman lost in thoughts of Rio
Ran aground.

Collisions:
From misinformation
Faulty maps
Blind faith.
Vessel off course collides with one on time
And in its proper place.

Broadsided:
Large wave
Caused by earthquake underneath the sea
Lives swept away
There's no defense
Not even steel . . . or wisdom.

Lousy weather:
Three men saved their lives by holding on
Waves topped with freezing spray.

These where the reasons ships went down
In January . . . Coos Bay, Oregon to Nome, Alaska.

Japan

Bushido Steel

Only the winter wind surrounds me
Soldiers do not come to look for death
Inside this cave.
My sword's calligraphy is perfect
Brush of steel
Red ink on white snow.

Netherlands

Amsterdam - Red Light District

Mental jailbreak from the puritanic laws made by the bourgeoisie
unending hordes of back-packed youth
throng happily along the tree lined sun-warmed summer's
narrow streets along a maze of glittering canals
reflecting dappled ripples
a Seurat of colors
leaf green, sky blue, golden sun
parade of small boats
sidewalks strewn with necklaces of bars, youth hostels
small two star hotels.

Live costumed manikins rap store-front windows
call to passers-by

"Hey baby, let me show you something you have never seen before."

Live sex shows glitter noonday neon above touts
who beckon while awaiting guided tour groups
sure to come along this evening
giddy with excitement.

Coffee shops abound for every taste and nationality
dispense bouquets of marijuana and hashish
cigarettes are not allowed.

Small groups are gathered joyfully at tables
rolling joints . . . discussing favorite blends
hushed conversations
music
smoothies
fresh fruit blended by young, tattooed baristas
Dutch Big-Easy.

Early Morning streets near vacant
lingering smell of beer
street cleaners wuzzing slowly by
an early morning prostitute
stands in her doorway
savoring the cool post-dawn.

What cause to leave this place
save winter's bleak and cold respite from joy
and jobs from which we can't escape.

Published: Northern Liberties Review - 2013

* Love Stories *

Four Feet Over Six Feet Under

Our lustful need for one another
Turned combustible
And she had teenage kids awake at her place
Mine was thirty miles away.
She led me to a grassy, well-kept graveyard
Where the night was still as death.

I asked, "Aren't you afraid here?"
It's the safest place in town, she said.
We made love on a marble slab at midnight
Undisturbed beneath a sickle moon
But I did not go back with her again
Into that quiet place
For reasons still uncertain.

Towards The End

Why did you open two? she asked.
Two what?
Bottles of wine, she said.
I didn't think you'd like what I was drinking.
Lifting my glass she said, It's bitter.

After a while she asked
You want the rest of mine?
Then left her drink to read a book
And watch TV.

Before she went to bed she called
Are you just going to sit there getting drunk
And staring at that candle?

Later that night
She woke up crying
And I had a dream about Christ
Nailed to a rocking chair grandfather's clock.

Solitude

After counting the hours
Of being alone
He found himself bankrupt
Making desperate payments
His heart could not cover.

* Labor Pains *

The Time of My Life

This summer afternoon
It's ninety-seven in the shade
And more
Inside my gear
White paper dust mask
Padded rubber on my ears
To stop some of the noise
A pair of safety glasses
Dark blue coveralls on top my clothing
Heavy leather gloves
Thick socks and steel toed boots.

Holding this powerful electric drill
Eight pounds of heavy metal
Spinning wire-brush wheel
A blur of blue and grey
Against the rust that has accumulated
On eight tons of angle iron
My job.

Eight hours inside a cloud of dark red dust
Fire storm of sparks
Steel bristles flying off
Go through my fabric armor
Into sweating skin
Dust makes it hard to breath
My glasses fogged by body heat

I watch the slow shop clock
Selling the time of my life
Six-fifty an hour.

Published: Pure Slush – Vol 5

The Bindery - First Night

I'm enthralled at first
In awe of this great space
The clatter of dark green machines
Metropolis of movement
Long conveyer belts metallic rattle
Forklifts as if in protest.

Night shift workers, 3 a.m.
Load pages into hoppers that are quickly emptied
Wanting more . . . insatiable
A warning buzzer sounds
Go faster . . . Faster!

Sweating on this concrete floor
Below the glare of bare fluorescent light
No mercy
Unforgiving hours
Between the pallet loads of printed pages
And the ever-hungry hoppers.

On my way home
At dawn
Ears ringing
Four more nights to go.

Boxboard

Temp job:
Alton Boxboard
Paper mill
Along the Mississippi River
Near Sr. Louis.

Paper spurts from great steel-grey machines that spin
Rolls thirteen-foot diameter
To trim rough edges
Take an inch or so from paper still too hot to touch
After a final pressing to desired thickness.
Spaghetti paper shavings, endless
Drop into an opening above.

My job—below
Beside a steel canal of flowing paper mush
Like oatmeal
Flowing into spinning shredders
Then around to be reduced by them once again.

When trimming starts
An endless white snake
Slithers through the hole
At high speed
Piles up fast
I have to hustle or get buried in it
Grabbing armfuls
Dropping them into the pulp canal
A strip adheres to the thick primal soup

Gets swept into the blades
Leave variety of paper cuts
My arms impossible to stay untangled from the mess
Too hot and humid for long sleeves
Eighty degrees and high humidity.

Discarded sheets of poster-board come down as well
Sail crazily
Short dance on overheated air
I do my best to keep up
With a growing mountain
Of white paper scrap
Then suddenly it stops.

Moment of peace
Some fifteen minutes
While they put a new roll on the shaft.
I think to sneak a rest
Lay down a couple minutes
On some sheets of cardboard
Still left on the floor
There's no one here but me
No windows
Just bare concrete walls
Inside this night shift hell.

Some wise guy throws a bucket filled with paper dye into the hole
I'm now light blue in color
Wide awake
Looks like a long night
Probably my last here.

* Birds of a Feather *

Crows

They go unnoticed overhead
Above the supermarket malls and cities
Countryside
Suburban fields and meadows
Watching
Airborne gangs dressed in black feather jackets
Fearless wise guys with a raucous comment
For the goings on below.

Bird of Perfection

Lives to be admired
From those outside a cage that holds no room for error
This fowl is always hungry, wanting more
Cannot be filled with anything but doubt
Its feathers ruffled by the winds of chance
Require constant preening
And high maintenance.

* Life On Earth *

The Alchemists

Just like the poor
We have been with you always
Need you to support us
Feed us
Serve us who possess wealth
Far beyond the means of spending
In a lifetime . . . Many lifetimes.

You who serve us
Fortunate to have the work we gave you
Welders, miners, teachers, doctors
Scientists and politicians
Soldiers to protect us, fight our wars
We sell the bullets.

Once called kings
We have now lost the weight of crowns
And any sort of obligation to the people
Governments and nations
We own palaces in many lands
Morphed into new age gypsies
Far beyond the reach of rules and taxes you cannot avoid.
We make the laws and politicians
Sure our cause is just for all
And most of all
For us.
Unknown by want
We are the alchemists
Who turn your sweat to gold.

Departure Implicit

Loretta lives across the street
Has cancer
Both of us are long of tooth
It happens
But at least I don't have cancer . . . yet
All of us carry the malicious cells within
Waiting for weakness
Less immune than yesterday.

But she's a tough old bird
From North Dakota
And offended doctors by refusing treatment costing thousands
Hair loss—nausea.
She takes pills for pain
Brian tumor headaches
Waiting for the end.
"I'm ready to go," she said.

Worked thirty years
Same job, same place
Small office manager/receptionist
Last week she finally gave it up.

Sometimes I think
Retirement has killed more of us than cancer.

Next Door

Apartment next to ours
Man verbally abuses wife
The walls are thin.

"Don't you ever talk to me like that!" he says
You bitch
God damn you!
I'm the husband here
What I say goes.
You understand that?"

There's no response that I can hear
But I can almost see her there
Unhappy and afraid
Eyes travel to a window
Wanting out.

"I asked you, do you understand!"
Her muffled voice
Response I barely hear
Then silence.

Saturday he's off somewhere
With friends
And she's at home
Minding their kid
He's seven.

"Don't you dare talk back to me!" she yells.
I am your mother
You are going to do exactly as I say!
You understand that?"
She demands an answer.
"Damn You."

I can hear no sound from him
But sense defiance
Slow to act
His turn will come.

Human Be-In   San Francisco 1967

The contact high of thirty-thousand people
Ginsberg, Leary, Richard Alpert, and Santana.
Gathering of tribes.
It seemed the world might change
On waves of personal empowerment
A crest of consciousness
The right to be ourselves
Sex, drugs and rock & roll
Ecology.

So many things.
Far East and Asian thought
Translations never seen before.
Hare Krishnas, Buddhism and Zen, Loa Tzu . . . The book of changes.
Hippies . . . Beatniks.
Woodstock without mud
A perfect day.
No cops
God was on time again
And we felt safe beside Hell's angels.

Escapade

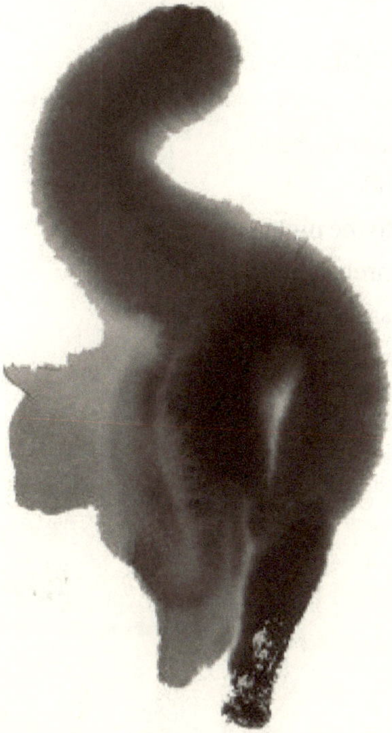

Cat slipped between my legs
As slick as silk
Into an open door and midnight
I should go and find him, but he will not come when called.
He wears a black fur coat not easy to discern.
It's late.

The lawns and shrubs have darkened
He is fast and I am slow, and tired
The feline will be out all night I guess
Come back tomorrow morning . . . hungry.

Early Morning Riser

Wakened at
Three thirty, early morning
Thup thup thup of rotors
Police helicopter overhead
Walk to the window
Looking out into the night
Fat beam of searchlight
Spidering across the neighborhood
Searching for what?
Or who?
I wonder
Did I lock the door?

We Are the People

"I have never taken a bus in my life—they're gross." Ivanka Trump

We Are the People
On the bus
The vast majority of us
Stand next to others we don't know

Strange faces . . . colors, smells, beliefs
The *other* people
Crowded on a pre-dawn morning
On our way to work
Then home again—and maybe later
Two days off
Or not.

We've known dismal, late-night rides . . . almost alone
Or waiting for the next one coming by
We do this without second thought
Necessity of life and
Lack of money, chauffeurs, maids
We *are* the maids, the chauffeurs
Collars blue and white
Making world go round
Clean up the mess—pay taxes
Fight the wars
For those
Who've never stood beside us.

Becalmed

He never feared the storm
Or loss of life at sea
But oh, those boredom hours
With blank horizon
Waiting for a breeze
Those endless days spent waiting
Polishing the brass.

Beginning of the End

Home at Last

Watching the dance of leaves
Tree on horizon bends to wind flow
Moment in tune with life
Beyond the plan of intellect

So good to sit here
By this window
Sun goes down
Soft pastel colors of the evening

Undulating scarf of crows fly home
I'm not sure where that is
No matter
End of day.

Time On My Hands

Backs of my hands
Grown wrinkled
Blue veins worm their way
Below now less resistant skin
Raise up
As if attempting to escape.

Age spots appear on fingers
As yet capable of grasping
Life.

Passing On Before and After

Going through old photos
Long departed mother left behind
A dusty album, black and whites
Approaching sepia with age.

Which ones to be discarded, or worth a passing on
To younger members of the clan
Who are these 1930's people?

Youthful Mom and Dad beside their parents
Relatives and family friends I never met
Pose awkwardly beside a vintage car
Converge around a Christmas dinner table.

Names now long forgotten

Gone forever
Nothing left beyond these faded camera shots.

Before too long someone will look at mine
and ask, "Who's that?"

Published: Taj Mahal Review

www.ingramcontent.com/pod-product-compliance
Lightning Source LLC
Chambersburg PA
CBHW050025170726
48282CB00025B/553
9789395224154